THE YUMS

In the freezer sat the naughty peas:

Julian, Paul, David and Fran

'What shall we do
when they open the bag?

Run away
as fast as we can'

'Let's first stick together in a big icy clump

That will annoy them for sure'

'They will have to make a big hole in the bag

then we can all fall onto the floor'

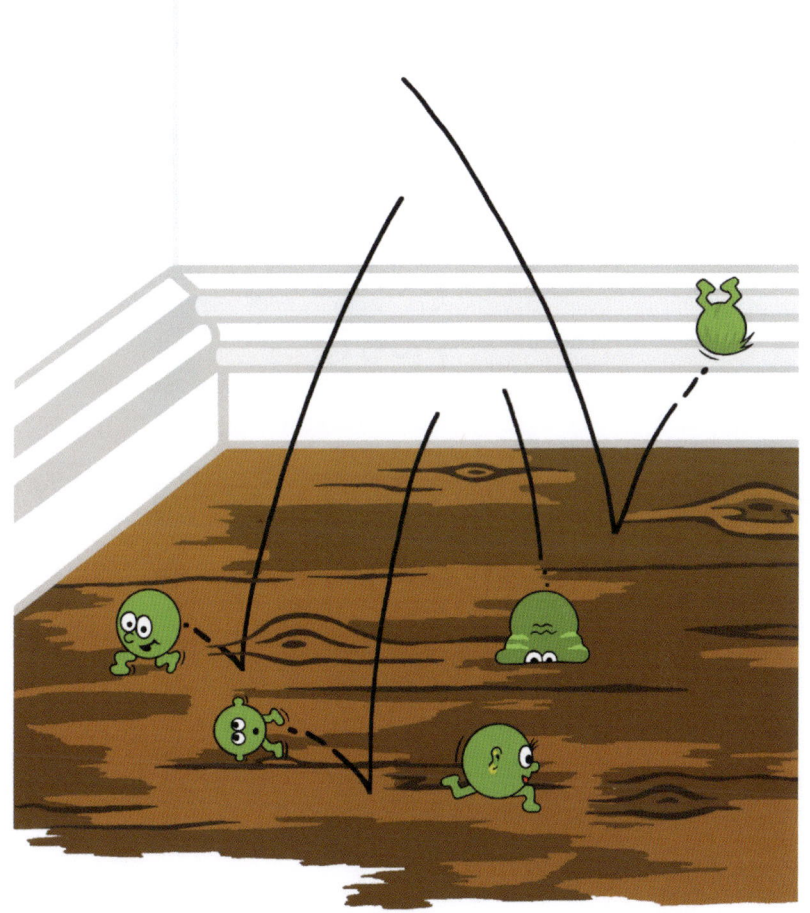

That was a good plan and a few peas escaped

but one got stuck in a crevice

There sadly he stayed to the end of the day

next to an old piece of lettuce

The icy lump was put in a pan

and the heat turned up very high

Mum bashed and squeezed to separate the peas

and Julian pinged right in her eye!

When served on a plate
Dave thought it was great

and started to play
'dodge-the-fork'

On some gravy he glided
with Sprout he collided

then hid himself under
some pork

The naughtiest pea was Paul
who was so proud
of being small

that he didn't mind at all
when *'Petit Pois'*
he was called

by a bully named
Mighty Meatball

Fran liked the games
some people play

sticking peas on the end
of their chips

They dunk them into
a dollop of sauce

which ends up
all over their lips

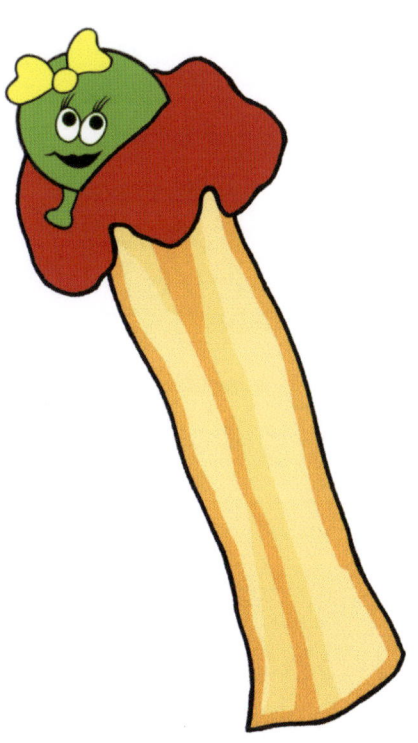

The best thing about being a Naughty Pea

is rolling all over the place

One might have just rolled under your chair

so you had better check just in case!

Created by Mary Ingram

Read about The Naughty Peas' friends ...

Apple

www.theyums.co.uk